WISDOM AND LOVE IN
SAINT THOMAS AQUINAS

Aquinas Lecture, 1951

WISDOM AND LOVE
IN
SAINT THOMAS
AQUINAS

Under the Auspices of the Aristotelian Society
of Marquette University

BY

ÉTIENNE GILSON

of the Académie française, Director of Studies and Pro-
fessor of the History of Mediaeval Philosophy, Pontifical
Institute of Mediaeval Studies, Toronto

MARQUETTE UNIVERSITY PRESS
MILWAUKEE
1951

Nihil Obstat

Gerard Smith, S.J., censor deputatus
Milwaukiae, die 17 mensis Septembris, 1951

Imprimatur

✠ Moyses E. Kiley
Archiepiscopus Milwaukiensis
Milwaukiae, die 2 mensis Octobris, 1951

PREFATORY

The Aristotelian Society of Marquette
University each year invites a scholar to de-
liver a lecture in honor of St. Thomas
Aquinas. Customarily delivered on the Sun-
day nearest March 7th, the feast day of the
Society's patron saint, these lectures are
called the Aquinas lectures.

In 1951 the Society had the pleasure of
recording a lecture by Étienne Gilson of the
Académie Française given Mar. 18.

Étienne Henri Gilson was born June
13, 1884 at Paris. He received his Agrégé in
1907 and became Docteur-ès-Lettres in 1913.
At the Sorbonne he was a pupil of Lucien
Levy-Bruhl who taught him historical method and suggested the study of Descartes'
borrowings from Scholasticism, a work
which led him to St. Thomas Aquinas and

the middle ages, the principal concern of his scholarly career. He was also a pupil, at the Collége de France, of Henri Bergson, "whose lectures" he recently said "still remain in my memory as so many hours of intellectual transfiguration," and whom he calls "the only living master in philosophy" he ever had.

In 1913 he taught at the University of Lille. During the first world war he was a machine-gunnery captain in the French army, was captured at Verdun and spent his time in a German prisoner of war camp writing and studying. After the war, in 1919, he joined the faculty of the University of Strasbourg. In 1921 he returned to the Sorbonne, this time to teach, and remained there until 1932 when he was elected to the Collége de France. He was Professor of the Philosophy of the Middle Ages at the Collége de France until 1950 when he retired. In 1929 he also became Director of

Studies and Professor of the History of Mediaeval Philosophy at the newly established Institute of Mediaeval Studies, Toronto, Canada, of which he is a co-founder and which in 1939 was raised to a Pontifical Institute by Pius XII. He continues in that position now.

Professor Gilson has held notable lectureships. In 1930 and 1931 he gave the Gifford Lectures at the University of Aberdeen, Scotland; in 1936-37 he gave the William James lectures at Harvard; in 1937, the Richards lectures at the University of Virginia, and in 1940, the Mahlon Powell lectures at the University of Indiana.

He is founder and director of *Archives d'Histoire Doctrinale et Littéraire du Moyen-âge* (with R.P.G. Théry) of which 16 volumes have been published since 1925; *Études de Philosophie Médiévale,* 35 volumes since 1921; *Études de Theologie et d'Histoire de la Spiritualité,* 9 volumes since 1934, and founder (with colleagues at the Pontifical Institute of Mediaeval Studies) of *Mediaeval Studies,* of which 9 volumes have been published since 1939.

Professor Gilson is a member of the French Academy, the Royal Academy of Holland, the British Academy, the American Academy of Arts and Sciences and the Pontifical Academy of St. Thomas Aquinas at Rome.

He has received many honorary degrees: Doctor of Letters (D.Litt.) from Oxford University; Doctor of Laws (LL.D.) from the University of Aberdeen, Harvard University and the University of Pennsylvania; Doctor of Philosophy (Ph.D.) from Rome, University of Milan and the University of Montreal.

He is president of the Franco-Canadian Institute, president of the Society of Catholic Authors at Paris, a member of the Secours Catholique International and of Pax Romana, before which he has lectured in Rome.

Professor Gilson entered the Conseil de la Republique, the upper house or senate of the present French government in 1946. He was technical adviser to the French delegation to the San Francisco Conference that same year, composing the French text of the Charter of the United Nations. He was also a French delegate to UNESCO, the United Nations Educational, Scientific and Cultural Organization, for which he also wrote the French text.

Professor Gilson has published the following volumes up to September 1951:

Index scolastico-cartésien, Paris, Alcan, 1913, ix and 355 pages. Out of print.

La Liberté chez Descartes et la théologie, Paris, Alcan, 1913, 453 pages. Out of print.

Études de philosophie médiévale. Collection des travaux de la Faculté des lettres de Strasbourg, Strasbourg, 1921, viii and 291 pages. Out of print.

La Philosophie de Saint Bonaventure, Paris, Vrin, 1st edition, 1924, 420 pages; 2nd edition, 1943, 483 pages; 1st edition translated under the title of *The Philosophy of Saint Bonaventure,* Sheed & Ward, New York, 1938, xiii and 551 pages.

Discours de la Méthode (Descartes) edited with commentary, Paris, Vrin, 1st edition 1925, 2nd edition 1939, text 78, commentary 490 pages.

Saint Thomas d'Aquin, (Les moralists chrétiens) texts and commentary, Paris, Gabalda, 6th edition 1941, 380 pages, translated under the title of *Moral Values and the Moral Life,* St. Louis & London, Herder, 1931, 329 pages.

Études sur le rôle de la pensée médiévale dans la formation de système cartésien, Paris, Vrin, 1930, 345 pages.

L'Esprit de la philosophie médiévale (the Gifford lectures of 1930-31) Paris, Vrin, 1st edition, 2 vols., 1932; 2nd edition, 1 vol., 1944, 447 pages; translated under the title of *The Spirit of Mediaeval Philosophy,* New York, Scribners, 1936, 1 vol., 484 pages.

Les Idées et les Lettres, Paris, Vrin, 1932, 300 pages.

Pour un ordre catholique, Paris, Desclée de Brouwer, 1934, 237 pages.

La Théologie mystique de Saint Bernard, Paris, Vrin, 1934, 251 pages; translated under the title of *The Mystical Theology of St. Bernard,* New York, Sheed & Ward, 1940, 264 pages.

Saint Thomas Aquinas, from *Proceedings of the British Academy,* Vol. XXI, London, Humphrey Milford, 1935, 19 pages.

Le Réalisme methódique, Paris, P. Tequi, 1936, 101 pages.

Christianisme et philosophie, Paris, Vrin, 1936, 168 pages, out of print; translated under the title of *Christianity and Philosophy*, New York, Sheed & Ward, 1939, 134 pages.

The Unity of Philosophical Experience (the William James lectures of 1937) New York, Scribners, 1937, 331 pages.

Mediaeval Universalism and Its Present Value (Harvard Tercentenary Conference 1936) New York, Sheed & Ward, 1937, 22 pages.

Reason and Revelation in the Middle Ages (the Richards lectures of 1937) New York, Scribners, 1938, 110 pages.

Héloïse et Abélard, Paris, Vrin, 1938, 252 pages.

Réalisme thomiste et critique de la connaissance, Paris, Vrin, 1939, 239 pages; soon to be translated into English.

Dante et la philosophie, Paris, Vrin, 1939, x and 341 pages.

God and Philosophy (the Powell lectures of 1940) New Haven, Yale University Press, and Oxford, Oxford University Press, 1941, 144 pages.

Introduction a l'étude de Saint Augustin, Paris, Vrin, 1st edition, 1929, ii and 352 pages; 2nd edition 1943, 352 pages; soon to be translated into English.

La Philosophie au moyen-âge, Paris, Payot, 2nd edition, 1944, 763 pages, soon to be translated into English.

Théologie et histoire de la spiritualité, Paris, Vrin, 1943, 27 pages.

Le Thomisme, Paris, Vrin, 5th edition 1945, 523 pages; 3rd edition translated under the title of *The Philosophy of St. Thomas Aquinas,* St. Louis, Herder, 1941; 362 pages; 5th edition soon to be translated into English.

Philosophie et Incarnation selon Saint Augustin (Conférence Albert le Grand, 1947), Montréal, Institut D'Études Médiévales Université de Montréal, 1947, 55 pages.

History of Philosophy and Philosophical Education (Aquinas Lecture, Fall, 1947) Marquette University Press, 1948.

L'Etre et l'essence, Vrin, Paris, 1948.

Being and Some Philosophers, Pontifical Institute of Mediaeval Studies, Toronto, 1949.

L'École des muses, Vrin, Paris, 1950.

Heloise and Abelard, (English translation) Regnery, Chicago, 1951.

Jean Duns Scot, Introduction à ses positions fondamentales, is in the process of being published by Vrin, Paris, 1951.

To these the Aristotelian Society takes pleasure in adding *Wisdom and Love in St. Thomas Aquinas.*

WISDOM AND LOVE IN
SAINT THOMAS AQUINAS

Da nobis, quaesumus, et quae docuit in-
tellectu conspicere, et quae egit imitatione
complere.

Proprium Missae S. Thomae de Aquino,
die VII Martii, MCMLI.

Wisdom and Love
In
Saint Thomas Aquinas

ALL students of philosophy are supposed to learn it from professors, who in their turn, are supposed to teach it. After learning it for three, four, or five years, some students at least are supposed to know philosophy so well that they are considered as qualified to teach it. If they do teach it, they have to follow programs, to use textbooks, to prescribe readings, to ask questions and to discuss answers to these questions; in short, they have to make sure that their own students learn philosophy in their turn and even, if possible, that they acquire the habit of discussing problems in a truly philosophical way. All this is necessary and, taken in itself, it is also excellent. Philosophy is undoubtedly a "learning" and, for this very reason, it has always been both taught and learned. Yet there was a time, in ancient Greece, when philosophy used to be quite something else, namely, a certain way and manner of life. It was, precisely, a life wholly dedicated to the pursuit of wisdom.

There are good reasons to fear that this second aspect of philosophy has lost its importance in the modern world. One might even wonder whether it is not in danger of being almost entirely forgotten.

The general trend of modern life is against the idea of philosophy as a way of life. Today, learning is sold by big department stores called colleges or universities where students can buy, as advertised, the kind of knowledge which suits their taste or answers their needs. Even their taste does not necessarily betray any very fervid inclination. I remember a university where students had to choose between philosophy and mathematics. It was surprising to see for how many of them the fear of mathematics was the beginning of wisdom. After attending so many examinations in philosophy in which students duly answered that philosophy was "the love of wisdom," I do not remember hearing a single examiner asking any candidate: "Well, do you love wisdom?" This would have been an unfair question. So long as the candidate knew what philosophy was, one could hardly ask for more. His private feelings about it were no one's business but his own, and to ask him if he was in love would have been not only beside the point but also positively indecent.

And yet, this was precisely the first question that Socrates would ask every new disciple that was brought to him: Are you in love with wisdom? Had the boy answered, for example: I am not sure that I am, but I am curious to learn it, Socrates would have advised him to seek one of those clever sophists who knew everything about philosophy without being themselves philosophers.

A similar treatment should be reserved for those among us who seem to imagine that "to be a Thomist" means to have an exhaustive knowledge of the complete works of Thomas Aquinas. This, of course, would not be a negligible achievement; but it would leave out something else, an achievement of an entirely different nature and yet one that is still more important. Thomas Aquinas has always granted to the Greek philosophers that wisdom was the highest possible knowledge. Since he was a theologian, theology was to him the supreme wisdom; but metaphysics itself was a wisdom, especially in as much as, intent upon the study of the first principles and causes, it helped theology in its work. Now, as a science through which man finds his way towards beatitude wisdom must be for him an object of love. Why, indeed, should we seek after wisdom unless we loved it? Rather how could we possibly acquire something which we do not desire to possess? A true Thomist, then, is a man who knows because he is a man who loves. There is, in other words, a moral side to the study of Thomas Aquinas.

Whichever part of his doctrine we consider, we are always in danger of overlooking half its truth. The peril is nowhere greater than at the point where we stress, and rightly stress, what is often called his "intellectualism." Thomas Aquinas was an intellectualist because he never relied on anything other than his intellect in order to know truth. Just as one can see only with his eyes, so he can know only with his intellect; but this truth should not lead us to imagine that man's intellectual life proceeds in him solely from the functioning of his intellect. All Thomists agree that, according to their common master, it is not the intellect that knows, but man through his intellect; and since man is many things in addition to his intellect, every time he knows, many other faculties co-operate in the making of his knowledge. The most important among them is the will. To forget this fact is also to overlook the further fact that there are practical conditions for the achievement even of speculative knowledge and that intellectual life involves problems of morality.

In order to restore the truth in its fullness, let us first remember that there are intellectual virtues, namely, wisdom, science and understanding. Because they do not fulfill the definition of virtue as adequately as the so-called "moral" virtues, that is, such virtues as perfect the appetite, we are inclined to think that the intellectual virtues are not *real* virtues. It seems to us that, when it *knows,* our intellect *does* nothing. But this is an illusion. When an intellect knows, it does the work of an intellect, and if, owing to some speculative virtue, this intellect does good work, it is a virtuous intellect. Now, in order to be a true Thomist, it is not enough to know that St. Thomas Aquinas had said this; a true disciple of Thomas Aquinas is one who, knowing this, absorbs it into the very fibre of his own being, that is, actually trains his mind to "understand" and to acquire "science" in the light of the first principles whose knowledge is "wisdom." These intellectual virtues are so truly real that, after a few questions and answers, any trained mind is able to recognize another trained mind which knows what it is to know. Many men are unaware of this, and there is not a single one of us who, as often as not, will not allow himself to speak as though he did not know what it is to know. Yet, just as to make good use of one's own intellect is an act of virtue, so to do the reverse is to yield to a vice. The speculative virtues confer upon our intellects the aptness for "the consideration of truth," which "is the good work of the intellect."[1]

To bring our conduct into conformity with this principle would make a great change in our lives. It should also make us better Thomists than we are, because it would cause us to become less different than we are from St. Thomas Aquinas. In the first place, it would make us realize that, since we never cease to think, we should never cease to know, nor to learn how to know. The speculative virtues of science and understanding should become in us, through constant exercise, so many permanent dispositions of the mind. What is a "cultivated mind" if not, precisely, a mind equipped with the largest possible number of sciences thus acquired, and, for this very reason, always ready to give intelligible answers to questions raised by the universe around us? Some of us, especially during those years when we are asked to study many sciences whose necessity is not always apparent, wonder if all the effort expended in such study is not a waste of time. We all want to learn something "useful", as if to learn were not always useful in order to know, which is not a means to a further end but an end in itself.[2] Man is a rational being whose ultimate end it is to achieve the perfection of his rational nature through the contemplation of absolute truth. In this sense, those speculative virtues which en-

able us to exercise intellectual acts are by
definition the highest of all human virtues,
because through them we are brought nearer
to our ultimate end. No true Thomist will
ever hesitate as to the moral value of a life
of studies. On the contrary, we should all do
the daily work of students, and among students I include the professors, with the
deep conviction that, since the speculative
virtues are the noblest of all, their acts can
be the most meritorious of all. Look at
Thomas Aquinas himself! He never did anything else than to read, to learn, to teach,
to write and to pray. But he did do it, and
far from doubting that to know was to do a
good work, he always maintained with Pope
Gregory the Great that "the contemplative
life has greater merits than the active life."[3]
The more meritorious of all good works is
the good work of the intellect.

If this means little or nothing to the life
of a professor, or to the life of his students,

then it is not easy to imagine what could possibly affect their lives. But let us be careful to note that, excellent though they be in themselves and absolutely, the virtues of the contemplative life are not meritorious by themselves. Man must acquire them in order that, through them, he may achieve the noblest kind of merit, but charity, justice and the other moral virtues are required in order to make the speculative virtues to be meritorious by conferring upon us the right use of their acts. In short, all due circumstances being present, the most meritorious of all acts is an act of contemplation of the highest intelligible object, when this act is informed by charity.[4]

If I could make clear to you the implications of this truth, I would also, by the same token, be pointing out one of the most un-Thomistic mistakes that a Thomist can make about the doctrine of his master. It should be agreed, among Thomists, that man knows through his intellect alone, not through his will, so that our will has nothing to do with the truth of a proposition. But there is more. According to Thomas Aquinas, our intellect exercises a spontaneity of its own, as is evident in its acts of reasoning. It argues from principles to consequences, or, conversely, from consequences back to principles, in virtue of its own intelligible light.[5] We all know those happy moments when, fully equipped with the science relevant to its present problem, our intellect proceeds to solving it practically without effort and so to speak, under its own power. In such cases, the will has nothing to do, except perhaps to prevent distractions, to keep the intellect upon its task when it weakens and, like an expert driver, to hold the wheel. But it should also be agreed among us that, just as man knows through his intellect, he desires to know through his will. The will alone does not know, the intellect alone does not desire. The tendency of the intellect towards truth, which is its end, is that of a nature, not that of an appetite, whose end is not the true, but the good, and which tends towards the true only inasmuch as truth itself is a certain good. Now it is a good thing for man to know truth. It even is the best possible of all good things, since it is in knowing God that man will achieve beatitude. In this sense, the desire to know truth is the very spirit that quickens our intellectual life, because it makes us desire to know what should be for us the final cause of all our cognitions.[6] Let us say then that the acquisition, the cultivation and the good use of speculative virtues require the co-operation of the will.

It is a well known feature of Thomism, that, in it, the will can command the acts of the intellect. If a certain sight strikes my eyes, I cannot not know the corresponding object, but if I do not wish to look at it, I can shut my eyes to it, just as, on the contrary, I can keep my eyes on it if I feel interested. In both instances, there is a choice, and this choice is the work of the will. The same remark applies to the cognition of intellectual objects. The will can always command the intellect to set to work or to rest; to look at a certain object or not to give it another thought; to exert its attention or else to relax it.[7] The presence or absence of intellectual virtues is irrelevant to our present problem. For moral virtues exercise a power of initiative because they are seated in the appetite or in the will, whereas the speculative virtues, precisely because they are seated in the intellect, have to be set in motion by the will in order that they may do their work. Thomas himself says this in terms of unsurpassable precision: "If a man possess the habit of a speculative science, it does not follow that he is inclined to make use of it, but he is made able to consider the truth in those matters of which he has scientific knowledge."[8] The inclination to make use of intellectual virtues is not to be found in the intellect itself; it lies in the will. And why should the will of a man turn his intellect towards a certain object rather than towards another one? It depends on the objects of this man's desire. If he be a true philosopher, what he desires is wisdom and, to the full extent that he thinks as a philosopher, his love of wisdom will be the mainspring which will set his intellect in motion and direct all its operations towards a successful achievement of his quest. There is no possible discussion about the authentic position of Thomas Aquinas on this point: the good philosophical life is the life of a philosopher whose intellect does good work owing to its speculative virtues, under the constant stimulation of a will which directs it towards perfect wisdom as towards the final cause of all its operations.

The ready objection to this conclusion is that it appears to turn Thomas Aquinas into an Augustinian. As often as not, those who raise this objection are the ones who rightly maintain that, in point of fact, Thomas *was* an Augustinian. Such confused positions cannot be clarified unless, precisely, our will intervenes and helps us, so to speak, to "make up our minds." For this is what we often have to do, not only in the practical matters of every day life but even in our speculative life as philosophers. The complete determination of an intellect by a certain object is limited to the evidence of this object, or rather, to what this intellect perceives of its evidence. Sense perception conveys with evidence to our intellects both the existence of perceived things and the accidental qualities which point out the essences of these things; but, even then, no adequate knowledge of these essences is at hand. When a scientist has to assent to some conclusion, even after bringing together all the relevant facts and checking against them his proposed solution, he still has to "make up his mind." No theory fits perfectly all the known facts. Moreover, there always remain more facts to come, and what proof is there that their discovery will confirm the proposed theory? Again, every scientific theory rests upon postulates, and it has happened in the past that apparently unchallengeable postulates have been profitably challenged. There are then many reasons why, at the hour of decision, the assent of an intellect should require the consent of the will. In Thomas Aquinas' own words:

"Some things which are apprehended do not convince the intellect to such an extent as not to leave it free to assent or dissent, or at least to suspend its assent or dissent because of some cause or other; and in such things, assent or dissent is in our power, and it is subject to our command."[9]

The same remark which applies to scientists also applies to philosophers, and even to metaphysicians. Absolute intellectual evidence has its limits. True enough, the first principles are necessarily evident both in their content and in their order, so that no human intellect can possibly be mistaken about them. In point of fact even a scientist who proudly proclaims that, as a scientist, he has no business with efficient causes or with final causes, will regularly get up every morning *because* he has to do so *in order to* be at his laboratory on time. The paradoxical fact is precisely that, while all men are naturally and necessarily infallible in their knowledge of the first principles, philosophers are not infallible *in what they say* about them. The truth of the case is that, as philosophers, men are more fallible than their own intellects; unless we prefer to say, that all men are necessarily right about the first principle, except the philosophers.

This is an obvious fact. How much time has it taken philosophers to put their finger on the first principle of the human mind? Look at Book I of Aristotle's *Metaphysics*. What an endless series of errors concerning the first principle is listed there! Was it Water? Or Fire? Or Air? Or Atoms? Or the Intellect? Or Ideas? Or Numbers? As Thomas Aquinas himself says, men have progressed towards truth so to speak *pedetentim,* that is, step by step and through the successive overcoming of many errors. How could we fail to see, as the mainspring of this collective quest for truth, a love of wisdom actively moving the human intellect towards an always purer light This was not a question of genius! Even Plato had not been completely right, and yet we still consider him to be one of the greatest human intellects of all times. Nor should we imagine that even the belated discovery of the first principles by Aristotle put an end to all metaphysical hesitation. If such had been the case, the history of philosophy would have come to an end with Aristotle's *Metaphysics*. But it did not. After Aristotle, there still was room for Thomas Aquinas, and mankind has had to wait the better part of two thousand years in order to learn from this greatest of all metaphysicians the full existential import of the word "being." Nor is this all. For it requires no less steady a will to keep truth, after it has been discovered, than it had required to discover

it. Because it needs to be found out, philosophical truth is always liable to get lost,
especially, one may say, with respect to first
principles, whose immediate intellectual evidence entails no exhaustive comprehension
of their content. True enough, being is the
first thing that falls into the intellect of man,
but it is also the last object which a philosopher may hope fully to comprehend and adequately to express. For those who have seen
it, it is evident that "being" is the first principle. It is also evident that every being is
that which it is, so that it cannot be, at one
and at the same time, both itself and something else. As to what it is to be "a being,"
the necessary answer is: it is "to be." All
this is certain, but what is it "to be"?

Aristotle has said[10] that this was already
a time honoured question in his own day;
today it is twenty-three hundred years older
than it was at the time of Aristotle, and it is

not yet a dead question, not indeed that truth has not yet been found, but because it has not been found by all. To agree that being is the first principle is not necessarily to agree about the nature of being. Is "being" a substance posited in existence by the efficacy of its cause? Or is "being" an essence to which existence is super-added as an accident? Or is the actual existence of being a *mode* of its essence? Or is existence the proper act of its own existence? Does "being" entail a real composition of essence and existence, or are these integral components of "being" distinguished from each other by a mere distinction of reason? Philosophers are so far from agreeing on these points that they do not always agree as to what Thomas Aquinas has said about them. The fact that there have been so many discussions among "Thomists" on the very meaning of the first principle is a sure sign that error is possible in what they themselves say about it. We know with certainty that being is the first among "the first principles," a fact which, by the way, should give us food for thought; for indeed, why does Thomas Aquinas so often speak of "first principles" in the plural? But many Thomists cannot even be brought to agree as to which is the second first principle: is it the principle of identity or the principle of contradiction? Personally speaking, it is evident to me that it is the principle of identity; but then my next question is: why do we not all agree on this point? When asked why it is that other metaphysicians do not agree with us on our interpretation of the first principle, we feel inclined to answer that the poor fellows are blind to evidence! But the very first condition which a proposition has to fulfill in order to be a "first principle" is, that "no one can possibly lie or be deceived about it."[11] Evidence is such knowledge to which no normal intellect can possibly be blind.

Why not rather admit that, because the first principles are supremely intelligible, these evident and necessary rules of the natural reason are to our intellects what sunlight is to the eyes of a bat? Metaphysicians are here groping their way in too much light, as they would in too much darkness. Metaphysics is a difficult science. In point of fact, Thomas says that it is the most difficult of all, and metaphysicians themselves know this fact but too well. So the wisest among them bide their time, but when they realize that time is running short, they too have to "make up their minds," not indeed out of impatience or in an arbitrary way, but, on the contrary, because their long-suffering love of wisdom is entitled to receive its reward. To what is evident in truth, our intellect cannot not assent; to what in it is not bindingly evident, and yet offers itself to the mind as the highest expression of rationality, our love demands that we assent as to the object of its desire. Nothing is more rational than such as assent: even where light is not perfect, not to assent to it is still to sin against the light.

This, at least, is a sin which Thomas Aquinas has never committed. Wisdom, to him, was not philosophy; it was not even theology; in its only perfect form, wisdom was Christ.[12] But he knew that to the Greeks, and to many other men after them, the highest known form of wisdom had been metaphysics, and he fully agreed that this science was the most perfect form of wisdom naturally acquirable by man. Thomas even knew why Pythagoras had preferred not to call himself a wise man, but rather "a lover of wisdom," because however much a man may try to achieve wisdom, he is always pre-

sumptuous in saying that he has achieved it.
A true philosopher is but a man who loves
wisdom for its own sake, because to love
it for the sake of something else is to be
a lover, not of wisdom, but of something
else. Thomas has been a lover of wisdom
under all its forms, at all its degrees, for the
sake of the absolute wisdom which according to St. Paul is Christ. It is the tirelessly
active love of Thomas Aquinas the man,
and not only his intellect, which still speaks
to us, even today in the colossal monument
of his *Opera Omnia,* written by a man who
died before the age of fifty. Were I asked
to sum up the main example given to us by
our master, I would answer: it is the example of a relentless will to know, coupled
with an absolute intellectual respect for
truth. Assuredly, his doctrine teaches the
primacy of contemplation over action, but
the prodigious labor of his life invites us

to think that Thomas has been Martha no less truly than he has been Mary. Let us make no mistake on this point. It took an uncommonly active life to write the *Summa Theologiae,* the Commentaries on Aristotle and on Peter Lombard, to say nothing of so many other treatises which it would be too long to mention; but the spirit which quickens all his works is still more instructive for us than their size, and it is here that we have to learn from him our lesson.

The first effect of Thomas' uncompromising love for truth is what I beg to call, since I am speaking of his philosophy, the *philosophical purity* of his doctrine. There are a hundred different ways for philosophical thought to be impure; it can indulge in literary facilities; in feelings, noble but out of place; in systematic thinking, which takes more interest in achieving self-consistency than in knowing reality. But all these im-

purities spring from the same source. Philosophy becomes impure as soon as it *is*
prompted by *any other motive* than the will
to know things exactly as they are and, in
knowing truth, to give it an adequate expression. This is precisely what Thomas
has always done, and a sure sign of the fact
is the nature of the oppositions which he
had to meet during his lifetime—to say
nothing of those which have risen after
his death. Some disciples of Augustine have
accused him of being too much a philosopher,
while at the same time some disciples of
Aristotle were accusing him of being too
much a theologian; but Thomas knew Augustine no less well than did the Augustinians,
and he knew Aristotle better than most of
the Aristotelians. Where what Augustine had
said was right, Thomas would say that
Augustine was right; and where Aristotle
had been right, Thomas would agree with

Aristotle. But in those instances when neither
Augustine nor Aristotle had been quite right,
Thomas would simply make them say what
was true, that is, what they themselves should
have said in order to be perfectly right. The
net result of this attitude could have been
foreseen; the Augustinians have said that
Thomas was betraying Augustine, while the
Aristotelians were saying that Thomas' own
philosophy was but a misrepresentation of
that of the philosopher. Very few among us
can imagine such a pure love of truth, that
is, a genius both capable of improving upon
Aristotle and Augustine, and yet disinter-
ested enough to credit them with his own
discoveries! Yet if we wish to be true disciples of Thomas Aquinas, each of us should
be ready, in the small measure of his capa-
city, to follow this example, that is obstin-
ately to hide behind truth. Truth is important, we are not. Why should we care about

the rest? Ever since the time of Plato, there have been noisy crowds to cheer the big show staged by the sophists in the market place; Thomas is the greatest among the few philosophers to whom it has been given to be both new and right; if we cannot be new, let us at least be right.

The only way for us to follow his example is, while learning his philosophy, to acquire with his help some of the moral virtues which go into the making of a philosopher worthy of the name. Those of us who teach his doctrine should always be careful to use him as a model not only of what to think, but also of how to think. While reading Thomas Aquinas, I sometimes remember a remark of A. N. Whitehead, which I beg to quote here because I am not sure that he has ever written it: "The first quality, for a philosopher, is to have a good temper." When he told me this, with that genial smile

which all his friends remember, Whitehead
certainly did not mean to say that a philosopher was not permitted to have a temper; he
meant to say that he should have none in
philosophy. *Doctrina,* Thomas says, *debet
esse in tranquillitate.* The mind of a philosopher should be at peace. Not to have a
temper in philosophy means never to become angry at an idea. It is, first of all, a
perfectly silly thing to do; but, above all,
the only business of a philosopher is to understand. The tremendous moral effort of
the will which is required from a philosopher in his quest for wisdom should have no
other objective than to shelter his intellect
from all the disturbing influences which
might interfere with the free-play of the
virtues of science and understanding. A
philosopher of good temper never attacks a
man in order to get rid of an idea; he does
not criticize what he is not certain to have

correctly understood; he does not lightly
turn down objections as unworthy of discussion; he does not take arguments in a more
unreasonable sense than is necessary from
their terms. On the contrary, since his business is truth and nothing else, his only care
will be to do full justice even to what little
there is of truth in every error. For a true
disciple of Thomas Aquinas the only way
to destroy error is to see through it, that is,
once more, to "understand" it precisely *qua*
error. There is only one thing which is worse
than error in philosophy; it is what some
people like to call its "refutation", when they
manfully condemn what they do not understand. Thomas never makes such mistakes.
What he discusses is what a man has said,
understood in the most intelligent sense of
which the words are susceptible. Once certain of its meaning, Thomas always refutes
the opinion of an adversary by ascribing to

it a place on a certain doctrinal scale of his own. All those who are at all familiar with Thomas Aquinas know the meaning of these scales; they do not classify doctrines according to their proximity to error, but according to their elongation from truth. Thus understood, even error makes sense, and because it is an act of understanding, its very rejection as an incomplete truth becomes a work of peace: *Doctrina debet esse in tranquillitate.*[13]

There is more in this than meets the eye. The unconditional respect for truth obliges us to look for it not only in the statements of our adversaries but also in those of our friends. This may appear to be an unnecessary piece of advice, but it is not. It means that we should never accept what a philosopher says for any other reason than the truth of what he says. "Respect ideas," Thomas says, "not because of the person who has ex-

pressed them, but rather for their reasonableness which alone makes them worth re-
membering."[14] A true Thomist will not
except Thomas himself from this rule. Let
the reasonableness of what he says justify
our admiration for him, but let not our admiration for him justify the reasonableness
of what he says. Naturally, after finding
him so often right, we are well founded in
expecting him to continue to be right; but
this feeling cannot justify a philosophical
approbation on our part. When we do not
understand clearly, or if we do not clearly
see how he is right, our only way to keep
faith with him is not to say: I do not understand, but he is right; the only true Thomistic
attitude is then for us to follow this other
piece of advice: "Strive to understand what
you read. Seek to clarify points of which you
are uncertain."[15] But some will say: what
if we cannot clarify these points? For such

men Thomas has still another piece of advice: "Do not concern yourselves with what is beyond your grasp."[16] I would however personally venture to add: do not be in haste to decide that metaphysics is beyond your grasp; the quest for wisdom is slow work, and the more brilliant students are not always the best philosophers. I imagine that several of the young Thomas' fellow-students could talk a great deal in class, whereas he himself was the "dumb ox"; and no wonder: while the others were talking, he was trying to "understand."

Among the philosophers whom we admire so much that we trust them implicitly, the most dangerous one is ourselves. Though it is perfectly human, the fact remains that when a man identifies himself with Thomas Aquinas and begins to argue as though to contradict him and to contradict Thomas were one and the same thing, he becomes positively dangerous. This, at least, is not to behave as a true Thomist, since Thomas himself utterly disliked presumption. He was by no means a skeptic, but he knew that "the inquiry of human reason for the most part has falsity present within it," partly because of "the weakness of our intellect in judgment", and partly because of "the interference of images."[17] Thomas has forcefully denounced those who, because they forget this fact, are liable to become self-assertive and to take themselves a little too seriously: "For there are some who have such a presumptuous opinion of their own ability, that they deem themselves able to measure the nature of everything; I mean to say that, in their estimation, everything is true that seems to them so, and everything is false that does not."[18] If it could be doubted that, in the mind of Thomas himself, philosophical life depends on moral virtue for its success, all doubt would be removed by his definition of the quest for wisdom: "A humble inquiry after truth."[19]

This is the true Thomas Aquinas, so different from those who mistake modesty for skepticism, and so like unto the wise man of Ecclesiasticus (XVIII, 7) who knew that "when a man has done, then shall he begin." Like his master Augustine, Thomas Aquinas is here inviting us to know "that the disposition to seek the truth is more safe than that which presumes things unknown to be known." To which Augustine had added these justly famous words: "Let us therefore so seek as if we could find, and so find as if we were about to seek."[20] Thomas Aquinas himself has clearly seen that this incomplete character of the most certain among our human certitudes was necessarily tied up with the present condition of man: "So long as a thing is in motion towards perfec-

tion, it has not yet reached its ultimate end.
But as concerns the knowledge of truth, all
men are always disposed as in motion to
their perfection and as tending to it; for
those who come after add certain things to
those which have been discovered by their
predecessors, as Aristotle likewise says in his
Metaphysics."[21] To imagine himself in another condition in relation to the knowledge
of truth would be, for a man in the present
life, to imagine himself already in possession
of his ultimate end.

In fact, no man is. And even among
those who humbly seek after truth, very few
find it by means of reason alone, not only
because few have the intelligence, the lei-
sure or the courage to undertake such a task,
but, above all, because "those who wish to
undergo such a labor *for the mere love of
knowledge* are few, even though God has
inserted into the minds of men a natural

appetite for knowledge."[22] Intellectual life, then, is "intellectual" because it is knowledge, but it is "life" because it is love. Unless we be among those few who wish to undergo such a life-long labor for the mere love of knowledge, we may well be brilliant students, great professors or even scholars thoroughly versed in the knowledge of Thomism; but we will not even have begun to become true disciples of Thomas Aquinas.

NOTES

Every commentary on Saint Thomas Aquinas should be read as an invitation to turn to his own writings. In order to enable the largest possible number of readers to form their own opinions as to the problems discussed in this lecture, I have used, whenever it was possible, the excellent and easily available English translations prepared by A. C. Pegis, President of the Pontifical Institute of Mediaeval Studies, Toronto. These translations will be found in the two following works: *Basic Writings of Saint Thomas Aquinas* (2 vols., New York: Random House, 1945) and *The Wisdom of Catholicism* (New York: Random House, 1949).

1. *Summa Theologica,* I-II, q. 57, a. 1, *Answer.* Quoted from A. C. Pegis, *Basic Writings of Saint Thomas Aquinas,* vol. II, p. 430.

The present lecture is an invitation to study, so to speak *in concreto,* the method actually followed by Saint Thomas Aquinas in his discussion of philosophical problems. An effort has already been made in this direction by J. Rimaud, *Thomisme et méthode,* Paris, G. Beauchesne, 1925. In a certain sense, all the publications of M.-D. Chenu, O.P., can be considered as so many contributions to the study of this important problem. Among these contributions, the most important one is his recent book: *Introduction a l'étude de Saint Thomas d'Aquin*, Paris, J. Vrin, 1950. Its conclusions about the theological method of Thomas Aquinas are often applicable to the philosophy which is included within Thomas' theology. Beyond its immediate historical aim and scope, this lecture implies a dogmatic invitation to the psychological study of actual intellectual life in the light of Thomas Aquinas' epistemological principles. Obviously, as disciples of Thomas Aquinas, our first duty is to recapture the true meaning of his principles, but merely to restate them would not be for us to fulfill our duty, neither towards him nor towards our own times. What we need is solid history, in order not to miss the real Thomas Aquinas, and even this will not be the work of any single historian, but that of all those among us who hold Thomas for their guide; but we also need a creative Thomism, in order to solve the problems of our own times in the light of the true principles of Thomas Aquinas. The concrete psychology of intellectual life is only one among these problems, but it is an important one. The best way, for a Thomist, to get others interested in Thomism, is to

show them that it "works." The *proof* of a
philosophy lies in the sole evidence of its principles, but the most manifest among the exter-
nal *signs* of its truth, is its speculative fecun-
dity. All Thomists are today challenged, by
the spiritual distress of the modern world, to
co-operate in making this sign visible to all.
A small part of the time we are wasting in
verbal controversies might be usefully spared
for this constructive task.

2. Taken in itself, knowledge is always good,
but even a good thing can be misused. On the
virtues which regulate the good use of knowledge, see notes 8 and 22.

3. *Summa Theologica,* I-II, q. 57, a. 1, *Answer;*
in *Basic Writings,* II, 430. Thomas Aquinas
has affirmed this point from the very beginning
of his career. Because contemplative life is
more noble than active life, the intellectual
habits, which perfect man in the life of contemplation, deserve the title of virtues much
more *(multo fortius)* than the moral habits,
which perfect man in the life of action: *In
III Sent.,* d. 23, q. 1, a. 4, qua 1, *sed contra.*
The same doctrine is to be found in *De Virtutibus in Communi,* art. VII. Note, in this text,
the following important precisions: 1, the in-

tellect and the will mutually encompass each other; 2, considered as preceding the will, the virtues of the intellect (understanding, science, wisdom) do not perfectly fulfill the definition of virtue, because they are not formally ordered to the attainment of the good, but materially only; 3, considered in the intellect taken as following the will, the speculative habits more truly deserve the title of virtues in as much as, through them, man is not merely able to know, but desirous to know; 4, intellectual habits are diversely related to the will: some of them hang on the will as to their use only, that is *per accidens;* which is the case of science, wisdom and art: some of them hang on will as receiving from it their principle, which is the case of the intellectual virtue of prudence, whose function it is to inquire into the best ways to achieve the good desired by the will, and to preserve it: and there is one speculative habit which receives from the will the determination of its very object, namely, faith, because "credere non potest homo nisi volens"; 5, all these habits can be said to be virtues in some way or other, but faith and prudence fulfill the definition of virtue more perfectly and more properly than science and wisdom; 6, *nota bene:* this does not entail that, taken in themselves, faith and prudence be more noble or more perfect habits than science and wisdom. This last remark agrees with the constant doctrine of Thomas Aquinas that, taken in itself, science is a higher speculative habit (i.e., a more perfect type of knowledge) than faith.

4. This superiority is due to the *intrinsic* superiority of knowledge as such. Knowledge is superior to all the other operations of man because it is through it that man can reach his ultimate end: "Consequently, to understand the most perfect intelligible object, God, is the greatest perfection of the operation *understanding*", *Contra Gentiles*, III, 25; in A. C. Pegis, *The Wisdom of Catholicism*, p. 304. Note, p. 305, the forceful expressions used by Thomas Aquinas: "the human *intellect* has a greater *desire* and *love* of the knowledge of divine things, as well as a *delight* in it, however little it can perceive divine things, than it has of the full knowledge open to it about the lowest realities." Cf. p. 307, on the natural *desire* of the intellect to know the cause of universal being. Some indications on the meaning of these expressions, and of similar ones, will be given later on, note 22.

5. The intellect is endowed with a spontaneity of its own. This spontaneity extends to the whole field of cognition as such. It is the intellect alone which proceeds from principle to conclusions, or which reduces consequences to the light of the first principles. In this sense, "reason commands itself, just as the will moves itself" (*Summa Theologica,* I-II, q. 17, a. 6, ad 1; in *Basic Writings,* II, 311. Cf. I-II, q. 9, a. 3, *Answer;* in *Basic Writings,* II, 253). In other words, through its knowledge of principles, the intellect moves itself (i.e., reduces itself from potency to act) to the knowledge of conclusions. This is simply to say that cognition as such is entirely and exclusively the work of the intellect. Yet, all the spontaneity of the intellect presupposes a twofold passivity: 1, towards its object, in this sense that the intellect is a passive power, which must be acted upon before it acts; 2, towards the will, in this sense that every cognition presupposes either the will to know or, at least, the consent of the will to the exercise of the intellect's power.

6. The agreement of Aristotle with the Gospel on this point has been noted by Thomas Aquinas himself in a text which each and every

Thomist should keep in mind: "Now the last end of man and of any intelligent substance is called *happiness* or *beatitude* for it is this that every intellectual substance desires as its last end, and for its own sake alone. Therefore the last beatitude or happiness of any intellectual substance is to know God. Hence it is said (Matt. V, 8): *Blessed are the clean of heart, for they shall see God;* and (Joh. XVII, 3): *This is eternal life, that they may know thee, the only true God.* Aristotle himself agrees with this judgment when he says that man's ultimate happiness is *speculative, and this with regard to the highest object of speculation." Contra Gentiles,* III, 26; in *Basic Writings,* II, 46. The reference to Aristotle (*Eth. Nic.,* X, 1177a 12-18) is a sure sign that, in the mind of Saint Thomas Aquinas himself, this was a *philosophical* truth, whose fullness had been revealed to men by the Gospel. On the indirect senses in which it can be said that the intellect "desires", see note 22.

7. *Summa Theologica,* I-II, q. 17, a. 6, *Answer;* in *Basic Writings,* II, 310-311. One of the main causes of verbal disagreement among Thomists on this point is that some of them speak of the act of cognition as exercized by

the intellect, while others speak of the act of cognition as exercised by man. Both points of view are equally legitimate in the doctrine of Thomas Aquinas, but they justify different answers to the same question. In speaking of "philosophers", we are dealing with "men", and it is manifest that, in the case of men who philosophize, the will is an important factor of their speculative behaviour. In so concrete a problem, one may be excused for speaking from personal experience. Many years ago, about 1924, a well known philosopher and theologian told me after one of my lectures on Thomas Aquinas: "I hate him! He is a evildoer." Hatred is not a philosophical argument. One of the silliest reasons quoted by adversaries of Thomism is also one among the most frequent ones; it is that *Thomists* are "unbearable," because they are self-assertive, intolerant, *etc.* The proposition: all Thomists are not saints, should probably be conceded, but what relation does it bear to the intrinsic truth of Thomism? There is a still more widely spread obstacle to the recognition of Thomism as a doctrine which every philosopher should discuss on its own merits; it is that, *as everybody knows,* Thomism is not worthy to be taken into account. Why? Twenty different answers will be given to this question: it is "mediaeval"; it is but a "theology"; it is nothing more than a restatement of Aristotle, who himself has already been refuted by Descartes; it is "scholastic", i.e., verbal; it expresses itself in a language that is "unintelligible" or, at least, not worthy of the trouble which one would have to take in order to understand it, *etc.* All these excuses are so many "prejudices"; they do not hang on reason, but on the will. Some of them are far from despicable. For instance, one may refuse to study Thomas because Augustine answers all his speculative needs; but, in this case, this is a presupposition, not a conclusion. Speaking *de facto,* all such attitudes are so many sins against the love of truth for its own sake, and whether they be inspired by indolence, or by a secret fear of truth, or by pride, or by mere stubbornness, or by straight cussedness, their origin ultimately lies in the will. Of course, it is quite possible, for a right minded philosopher, to find purely speculative obstacles to the acceptance of Thomism. When such is the case, the problem is of a purely philosophical nature; its solution rests with the intellect, not with the will.

8. *Summa Theologica*, I-II, q. 57, a. 1, *Answer;*
in *Basic Writings*, II, 430. The same doctrine
is maintained in *De Virtutibus in Communi*,
art. VII, *Answer:* "non enim ex hoc quod
homo habet scientiam, efficitur volens consi-
derare verum, sed solummodo potens; unde et
ipsa veri consideratio non est scientia in quan-
tum est volita, sed secundum quod directe
tendit in objectum." The same conclusion applies to art, which is a habit of the practical
intellect. An artist can make works of art, but
his inclination to make them is not in his art,
it is in his will. There is no more philosophical
life in a lazy philosopher than there is artistic
life in a lazy artist. Cf., in the same text:
"non enim per hos (habitus) homo ad hoc
perficitur, ut homo eis velit uti, sed solum ut
ad hoc sit potens." See also ad 5. This is
why, while the knowledge itself of the truth
is always good, the desire in the pursuit of the
knowledge of truth may be evil, whether because it becomes immoderate (*Sum. Theol.*, II-
II, q. 166, a. 2), or else because it is misdi-
rected (*Sum. Theol.*, II-II, q. 167, a. 2). An
intellectual virtue, which is always good in itself, is always distinct from the act of the
appetitive power which directs its use or its
application (*Sum. Theol.*, II-II, q. 166, a. 2, ad

2). The virtue which moderates the mind's application to knowledge is "studiousness": *Sum Theol.*, II-II, q. 166, a. 1, *Answer*.

9.   *Summa Theologica,* I-II, q. 17, a. 6, *Answer;* in *Basic Writings,* II, 311. This is eminently true of the virtue of faith, but the generality of the formula is absolute: as soon as there is any reason for the intellect to withhold its assent to a conclusion, "assensus ipse vel dissensus in potestate nostra est et sub imperio cadit." The whole problem then is to know how far absolute intellectual evidence does extend? *De jure,* it extends to all that which can be necessarily related to the evidence of the first principles; *de facto,* it extends to that which is actually so related. The virtue of *docilitas* precisely consists in the good will of the pupil to open his mind to the light of teaching; to make himself receptive of truth even before it has been evidently seen by his intellect; at least, it is the will not to behave as a *protervus*. Psychological enquiries into these problems would prove fruitful. The whole concrete behaviour of man towards truth could be usefully analyzed in the light of the general rule which is here laid down by Saint Thomas Aquinas.

10.   Aristotle, *Metaphysics*, Z 1, 1028b 2-7:
"And indeed the question which was raised of
old and is raised now and always, and is always the subject of doubt, viz., what being is,
is just the question, what is entity *(ousia)* ?";
quoted from W. D. Ross' translation *(The
Works of Aristotle,* vol. VIII, 10028 b). We
have taken the liberty to change the last word,
and to substitute *entity* for *substance.* Cf. J.
Owens, *The Doctrine of Being in the Aristotelian "Metaphysics",* Pontifical Institute of Mediaeval Studies, Toronto, 1951, Ch. VIII.

11.   Our whole argument is *de facto.* The only
way to disprove it would be to turn down the
massive historical evidence, attested by Thomas
Aquinas himself, of the factual disagreement
which obtains among philosophers as to the
nature and import of the first principles of
human knowledge. The more certain one is
that Thomas Aquinas is evidently right on this
point—and, personally, we are absolutely certain of it—the more concerned he should be
with the paradoxical situation in which we are:
if the being *"habens esse"* of Thomas Aquinas
is an immediate and necessary evidence of the
human intellect, which it is, how is it that so
many philosophers fail to see its evidence? How

is it that so many men are actually deceived about a proposition which, since it is about the first principle, should be necessarily and evidently grasped by each and every human intellect? (*In Metaph.*, IV, lect. 6; Cathala, n. 537). Facts alone are responsible for the existence of the problem, and no one of us should imagine that he will give it a completely correct answer, so to speak, single handed; but the refusal to face *any* real problem would be, on our part, about the worst conceivable betrayal of Thomas Aquinas.

12.   "Inter multas sententias quae a diversis prodierunt, quid scilicet esset vera sapientia, unam singulariter firmam et veram Apostolus protulit dicens *Christum Die virtutem et Dei sapientiam, qui etiam factus est nobis sapientia a Deo.*" Thomas Aquinas, *In Sent.*, I, Prologus. The reference to Saint Paul is, *I Corinth.* 1, 26 and 30.

13.   Thomas Aquinas, *In Joannis Evangelium,* cap. 13, lect. 3, n. 1; in the Vivès edition, vol. 20, p. 209. The same doctrine is also to be found in *Contra Gentiles,* I, 4, and Aristotle, *Physics,* VII, 3, 247b 9 (See A. C. Pegis, *The Wisdom of Catholicism,* p. 295). This is why, Thomas says, "in youth, when the soul is

swayed by the various movements of the passions, it is not a suitable state for the knowledge of such lofty truth."

14. Thomas Aquinas, *A Letter on the Rule of Life of a Scholar*, translated by Clare C. Riedl (Milwaukee; Marquette University Press, 1937)

15. *Ibid.*

16. *Ibid. Cf. Eccli.* 3, 22, as quoted by Thomas Aquinas in *Summa Theologica*, II-II, q. 167, a. 1, *Answer*, where this fault is listed among the various forms of a definite vice: curiosity.

17. *Contra Gentiles*, I, 4; in A. C. Pegis, *The Wisdom of Catholicism*, p. 296.

18. *Contra Gentiles*, I, 5; in A. C. Pegis, *The Wisdom of Catholicism*, pp. 297-298.

19. *Ibid.*, p. 298. This, Thomas says, is one of the reasons why God has fittingly proposed to men for belief some truths which the human reason cannot investigate: it curbs presumption.

20. Augustine, *De Trinitate*, IX 1; Migne, *Pat. Lat.*, vol. 42, col. 961. This text eminently applies to the case of a Christian seeking to "understand" what he believes about the mystery of the Trinity: "Certa enim fides utcumque inchoat cognitionem; cognitio vero certa non

perficietur, nisi post hanc vitam, cum videbi-
mus facie ad faciem." But the remarks of
Augustine apply no less well to the quest of
wisdom as such, the more so as, according to
Thomas Aquinas himself, perfectly to reach
it is impossible to man in this life. See the
text quoted in the following note.

21.   Thomas Aquinas, *Contra Gentiles,* III, 48;
in A. C. Pegis, *The Wisdom of Catholicism,* p.
313. (Cf. Aristotle, *Metaphysics,* I, 1, 993a
12). Note the intentionally careful expressions
used by Thomas Aquinas in the next lines:
"Since, therefore, the highest felicity of man
in this life seems to consist in the speculation
through which he is seeking the knowledge of
truth. . ." *etc.*

22.   *Contra Gentiles,* I, 4; in A. C. Pegis, *The
Wisdom of Catholicism,* p. 295. This "natural
appetite for knowledge" inserted by God into
the "minds" of men can be understood either
as the natural tendency of the intellect towards
truth, or as a natural appetite of the will which
cannot not desire knowledge. Ferrariensis
favours this second interpretation, in his commentary on *Contra Gentiles,* I, 4, Leon. edit.
vol. XIII, p. 12: "ideo dicendus est iste ap-
petitus esse naturalis quidam actus voluntatis,

quo voluntas in propositam sibi cognitionem
fertur ita quod in oppositum ferri non potest."
Both interpretations are true; the second one,
which is also the deeper one, is confirmed by
Sum. Theol., I-II, q. 10. a. 1, *Answer,* where
Thomas says that the will does not desire the
good in general only, "but also that which per-
tains to each power, and to the entire man,"
such as, for instance, "the knowledge of truth,
which befits the intellect, and to be, and to
live. . ." *etc.* This desire for knowledge is so
clearly seated in the appetite that it stands in
need of being regulated by a "moral" virtue,
which is "studiousness" (see above, note 8).
The main effect of this virtue is to exercise a
certain restraint on our natural desire to know
things. As it prevents this desire from growing
immoderate, studiousness is a subordinate virtue related to the principal virtue of temper-
ance. Secondarily, it designates our aptness to
overcome the labour which is required for the
acquisition of knowledge (*Sum. Theol.,* II-II,
q. 166, a. 2, *Answer,* and ad 3). The natural
appetite for knowledge, of which Thomas
speaks in *Contra Gentiles* I, 4, must therefore
be understood, not only as a natural tendency
of the intellect toward truth, but also as a part
of the desire of man for the good in general.

The Aquinas Lectures

Published by the Marquette University Press,
Milwaukee 3, Wisconsin

The Nature and Origins of Scientism (1944) by Fr. John Wellmuth, S.J., Chairman of the Department of Philosophy, Xavier University.

Cicero in the Courtroom of St. Thomas Aquinas (1945) by the late E. K. Rand, Ph.D., Litt.D., LL.D., Pope Professor of Latin, *emeritus*, Harvard University.

St. Thomas and Epistemology (1946) by Fr. Louis-Marie Régis, O.P., Th.L., Ph.D., director of the Albert the Great Institute of Mediaeval Studies, University of Montreal.

St. Thomas and the Greek Moralists (1947, Spring) by Vernon J. Bourke, Ph.D., professor of philosophy, St. Louis University, St. Louis, Missouri.

History of Philosophy and Philosophical Education (1947, Fall) Étienne Gilson of the Académie française, director of studies and professor of the history of mediaeval philosophy, Pontifical Institute of Mediaeval Studies, Toronto.

The Natural Desire for God (1948) by Fr. William R. O'Connor, S.T.L., Ph.D., professor of dogmatic theology, St. Joseph's Seminary, Dunwoodie, N. Y.

St. Thomas and The World State (1949) by Robert M. Hutchins, Chancellor of The University of Chicago.

Methods in Metaphysics (1950) by Fr. Robert J. Henle, S.J., Dean of tthe Graduate School, St. Louis University, St. Louis, Missouri.

Wisdom and Love in St. Thomas Aquinas (1951) by Étienne Gilson of the Académie française, director of studies and professor of the history of mediaeval philosophy, Pontifical Institute of Mediaeval Studies, Toronto.

First in Series (1937) $1.00; all others $2.00
Uniform format, cover and binding.